BAPTISM: Experi
refreshing tim

Copyright © 2021

By Sunday Olalekan Akodu

sundayakodu@yahoo.com

All rights reserved

All scripture quotations are from the Authorized King James version of the Bible.

CONTENTS

Dedication	3
Acknowledgement	4
Introduction	5

Chapter One

Salvation	12

Chapter Two

Water Baptism	38

Chapter Three

Sanctification	52

Chapter Four

Holy Spirit Baptism	65

DEDICATION

I dedicate this book to God, the Father, who sent His Son to redeem us from sin and His Holy Spirit to empower us.

ACKNOWLEDGEMENT

I acknowledge everyone that has been redeemed by the blood of the Lamb, sanctified and filled with the Holy Spirit showing forth the powers of God upon the Earth. May the Lord continue to strengthen us in His service to mankind.

I also specially appreciate those that the Lord has used to support my Ministry. May the Lord bless them all.

I also appreciate you, the readers of my books. May you continue to experience the power of God around you always.

INTRODUCTION

"Jesus answered and said unto him, verily, verily, I say unto thee, except a man be born again, he cannot see the Kingdom of God. Nicodemus saith unto him, how can a man be born when he is old? Can he enter the second time into his mother's womb and be born? Jesus answered, verily, verily, I say unto thee, **except a man be born of water and of the Spirit**, he cannot enter into the Kingdom of God. **That which is born of the flesh is flesh, and that which is born of the Spirit is spirit**". John 3:3-6 KJV

Jesus was telling Nicodemus what he needed to do for him to be saved. Jesus told him that he needed to be born again and in verse 5 of John chapter 3, the Lord explained further to him since he could not comprehend the meaning of being born again. Jesus said he needed to be born of water and of the Spirit. Then in verse 6, He explained further that he that is born of the flesh is of the flesh and he that is born of the Spirit is of the spirit.

People always interpret being born of water as water Baptism but the Lord was not referring to water baptism in the above scripture. Jesus spoke of two births in verse 5: being born of water and being born of the Spirit. Then in verse 6, He spoke again of two births to explain further what He meant in the previous verse so that Nicodemus could understand better: being born of the flesh and being born of the Spirit. The birth of water is the same as the birth of the flesh.

Jesus was telling Nicodemus that anyone that will enter into heaven must first be given birth into the Earth which is the birth of water, the birth of the flesh, a physical birth then he/she then have a rebirth on the Earth, the birth of the Spirit, that is, become born again. Anyone that has seen the Kingdom of God has entered into it. Nothing defiling shall in any way come near Heaven.

"Before I formed thee in the belly I knew thee: and before thou comest forth out of the womb I sanctified thee and I ordained thee a prophet unto the nations." Jeremiah 1:5 KJV

Before we were physically born into the Earth by our mothers, we had existed as spirit-beings. We saw God telling Jeremiah that He knew him before he was formed in his mother's belly. That, Jeremiah had existed as spirit-being before he was birthed physically on the Earth and has been predestinated for a purpose. You could have a better understanding of this in my book titled "Fulfilling the purpose of God: becoming who God has created you on the Earth".

In view of the above, to enter into Heaven, you must first be physically born into the Earth which is the birth of water, the same as the birth of the flesh, then you have a rebirth, become born again, the birth of the Spirit. It is our work on the Earth after salvation that will make us to get to Heaven.

People on the sick bed who gave their lives to Christ before they died will enter into Heaven without water baptism because they have fulfilled the requirements needed to enter into Heaven. They have been born of water, the physical birth and also born of the Spirit, the rebirth. If it is water baptism that John 3:3-6 referred to, then such sick people at the points of death who had accepted Jesus Christ will not make it to Heaven.

Water Baptism is important. It is when you undergo the spiritual things with understanding, that you benefit from the blessings such entails. One of the reasons people are not blessed is because they don't have the understanding of what they do, some are doing the spiritual tasks as if they are forced by their Church to do them, so no how they will have the blessings of partaking in such tasks. You must do every spiritual task with the willing heart and with understanding of what you are doing. God is not a task master.

"And ye shall know the truth and the truth shall set you free". John 8:32 KJV

You need to know the truth for you to be blessed by God. One of the major tools of the devil this end time is preventing people from having deeper knowledge of the word of God. It is your knowledge of the word of God that shall make you victorious at all times over the devil and his forces.

There are two kinds of Baptism: Water Baptism and the Holy Spirit

Baptism. These two shall be discussed in this book.

Read through this book with total sensitivity in the spirit. I believe you shall experience a refreshing time through the outpouring of the Holy Spirit upon you. Release yourself totally to the Holy Spirit and you shall have a testimony to share to the glory of God. Be blessed.

CHAPTER ONE

Salvation

"Jesus answered and said unto him, verily, verily, I say unto thee, except a man be born again, he cannot see the kingdom of God." John 3:3 KJV

"But seek ye first the kingdom of God and his righteousness; and all these things shall be added unto you." Matthew 6:33 KJV

Salvation is the beginning of our walk with God. It is salvation that transforms us from the kingdom of darkness into the kingdom of light. It is salvation that will qualify us to receive abundant blessing from heaven. It is salvation that will make us to be children of God.

"But as many as received him, to them gave he power to become the sons of God, even to them that believe on his name: Which were born not of blood, nor of the Will of the flesh, nor of the Will of men, but of God." John 1:12-13 KJV

When one receives Jesus as he/she confesses his/her sin and accepts Jesus as his/her Lord and personal saviour, he/she has become a child of God. His/her spirit and soul have been renewed. You are now a new creature, the old things have passed away and all things have become new.

As we have seen in the Introduction, until we are born of the Spirit after we have been born of the flesh (water) before we can be saved. If you are not yet saved, then this is an opportunity to make your way right with your maker. Let us pray:

Ask God for the forgiveness of your sin as you confess them before God.

Ask the Lord Jesus to come into your life and become your Lord and saviour.

Believe in your heart that your prayer has been answered.

You can now pray this prayer:

Lord Jesus, forgive me my sin and redeem me from the kingdom of darkness into the kingdom of light through your blood which you shed on the cross of Calvary. Make me a new creature today and make the old things to pass away. I confess You as my Lord and saviour. Come into my heart and direct my life forever, in Jesus name I have prayed.

As you have prayed this prayer in faith, you are now born again. Pray and study the word of God regularly, so that you can grow in faith. Also declare your salvation boldly to people, so that they can know that you are now a new creature. Attend a bible believing Church and participate in their programmes so that you can grow spiritually. You are now welcome to the winning side.

As you have received Jesus Christ today, He has given you power to become a child of God. You are now led by the Holy Spirit. What a day today. Heaven is happy about this your decision today. Write today's date down in a place for you to remember your date of new birth. The way you know if your prayer of salvation has been heard by God is having peace in you. If you have peace in you after the above prayer, then you are truly saved. My prayer for you is that: May the Lord make you a pillar in His temple so that you shall be His own all through your life, in Jesus name, Amen.

I was saved by the Lord Jesus in 1991 in my secondary school when I was in senior secondary school one at Bolade Grammar School, Oshodi as my classmate, Chidiebere, preached to me. What a great day in my life. The Lord has upheld me in Him since then. To God alone be all the glory.

If you are already saved, then hold fast unto your salvation, do not allow the devil to take it away from you because it is a precious gift.

If you are lukewarm or have totally lost your salvation, it's time for you to get restored back today. Let us pray:

Ask God for the forgiveness of your sin as you confess them before God.

Ask Him to restore you and uphold you in this restoration all through your life.

Believe with your heart that your prayer has been answered.

You can now pray this prayer:

Lord, You said whosoever that shall call upon You, You will not cast away. My Lord and my saviour, I return back unto you today, let your power of restoration fully restore me back unto You today. Let me begin to fulfill Your purpose for my life from today. Make me a pillar in Your temple forever, in Jesus name I have prayed, Amen.

Hurray! You have been restored today. Continue to grow in faith. What a day.

Indwelling Anointing

"And I will pray the Father and he shall give you another comforter, **that he may abide with you forever;** even the Spirit of truth; whom the world cannot receive because it seeth him not, neither knoweth him: but ye know him; **for he dwelleth with you and shall be in you**". John 14:16-17 KJV

"But ye are not in the flesh but **in the Spirit, if so be that the Spirit of God dwell in you,** now if any man have not the Spirit of Christ, he is none of His". Romans 8:9 KJV

We are saved through the Holy Spirit convicting us of our sin and thereby purifying us by which we become a living soul. At this point of our new birth, the Holy Spirit comes into us and dwells in us by which we become of the spirit and no more of the flesh.

Every believer has this indwelling anointing in him/her which abides within him/her. The indwelling anointing is to build us up.

It is the indwelling anointing i.e. the coming of the Holy Spirit upon one during salvation that makes one to be born of the Spirit. This is the new birth, born again. As we continue to fellowship with the Holy Spirit, this new birth is retained in us and we increase in the anointing. If we continue to the end in this fellowship with the Holy Spirit, then we shall enter into Heaven at the end of our race on the Earth. Therefore, continue to walk in the spirit and be totally obedient unto God because it is whoever that endured to the end that shall be rewarded.

The indwelling anointing is a measure of anointing that comes upon a believer when he/she is saved. The anointing increases as he/she grows in the Lord. At salvation, one is a baby in the Lord like a child physically born into a family. Babies are fed with milk till they grow up and begin to eat strong bones. A child of God grows in faith beginning as a baby and as he/she continues in the fellowship with the Holy Spirit through prayer and studying of the Bible in total obedience unto God, will grow into matured child of God who can eat strong bones. Every child of God begins as a babe before growing into maturity. May the Lord nurture you every moment, in Jesus name, Amen.

Fruit of the Spirit

"But the fruit of the Spirit is love, joy, peace, longsuffering, gentleness, goodness, faith, meekness, temperance: against such there is no law". Galatians 5:22-23 KJV

The indwelling anointing that comes upon one at the point of salvation bears 9 fruit of the Spirit in someone. Someone that is truly born again must have a measure of the 9 fruit of the Spirit upon him/her at the point of his/her salvation. If any of the fruit is lacking, then his/her salvation is not complete. As I have said, we increase in anointing as we grow in the Lord, but at the point of salvation, a measure of anointing is upon us which bears a measure of the 9 fruit of the Spirit in us. The measure of the anointing increases as we grow in the Lord and also increases the measure of the 9 fruit of the Spirit in us. If one does not have a measure of the 9 fruit of the Spirit in one at the point of one's salvation, then the salvation is not complete.

Love:

"And Jesus answered him, the first of all the commandments is, hear, O Israel, the Lord our God is one Lord: And thou shalt love the Lord thy God with all thy heart and with all thy soul and with all thy mind and with all thy strength: this is the first commandment. And the second is like, namely this, Thou shalt love thy neighbour as thyself. There is none other commandment greater than these". Mark 12:29-31 KJV

"Love worketh no ill to his neighbour: therefore love is the fulfilling of the law". Romans 13:10 KJV

The 10 commandments are summarised in love: the love for God and the love for our neighbours. Paul also said love is the fulfillment of the law. Therefore, we are called to love. You can only minister effectively to people you love. Jesus has compassion for people, which makes Him to always want to heal them (Matthew 14:15-21).

Every child of God is expected to have divine love in him/her.

If a child of God cannot show forth love, there is problem with his/her salvation.

It is this divine love that builds you in the spiritual life as you want to please God who has redeemed you from the world. One of the ways to know if truly anyone has truly been saved or not is to see if divine love manifest in him/her.

"He that loveth not knoweth not God; for God is love".   1John 4:8 KJV

The above scripture says anyone that does not love, does not know God. This means that if you are a child of God, then you must show forth love. If love is lacking in you, then you are not saved. All the patriarchs are men of love. The early believers shared their things among themselves such that none lack among them (Acts 4:34-37). Moses loved the children of Israel that he interceded for them whenever God was angry with them. Also, David, Solomon, Samuel etc loved their people. We saw the great exploit the patriarchs did because they were men of love.

Peace:

"These things I have spoken unto you that in me ye might have peace. In the World ye shall have tribulation: but be of good cheer, I have overcome the World". John 16:33 KJV

Peace is a state of being calm or quiet. Jesus is the Prince of peace. Peace could only be given by God because it is a fruit of the Spirit (Galatians 5:22). For you to be able to experience the presence of God around you, you need to be at peace. You need peace to be able to be in tune with heaven. A restless person cannot be in tune with heaven.

Peace occurs inside (within) one even if there is no physical manifestation around one. Peace is of the mind. In the midst of great storm, one can still be at peace inside (within) one. Peace is the beginning of the manifestation of the power of God around one. You must first be at peace before you can experience the presence of God around you. It is peace that births faith which then produces the manifestation. Peace is very important to experience the manifestation of God around you.

Peace is a proof that God is with you. If you have peace around you, it's a sign that you are on the right path.

At salvation, one of the ways you know that truly you have been saved after your prayer of confession of sin and acceptance of the Lord Jesus as your Lord and savior is peace. If you have peace in you after the prayer, then you are saved but if you do not have peace within you, then the salvation is not complete. As soon as you are born again, the peace of the Lord will come into you. As I have said, if you didn't have the peace of the Lord in you after your confession of sin, the salvation is not complete. May be you didn't truly confess your sin before God. Go back to God for your salvation and He shall surely save you and His peace shall be upon you.

Joy:

You experience joy as a result of what makes you happy i.e. as a result of a manifestation. As peace is the beginning of experiencing the manifestation of the power of God, joy is the result of the manifestation. Therefore, peace is the beginning and joy is the end.

After every victory, you become joyous and the joy results in praise to thank God for what He has done. It is God that makes us joyful (Psalm 16:11).

At salvation, the peace of the Lord that springs forth in one produces joy in one.

As all the virtues from God are in measures, so also is joy. There is a moderate joy (Psalm 126:5), a great joy (Luke 2:10) and an exceedingly great joy (Mathew 2:10).

Faith:

"And Jesus said unto them, because of your unbelief: for verily I say unto you, if ye have faith as a grain of mustard seed, ye shall say unto this mountain, remove hence to yonder place and it shall remove and nothing shall be impossible unto you". Matthew 17:20 KJV

At salvation, a measure of faith comes upon you which makes you to walk with God in the Spirit because you are no more of the flesh but of the Spirit. It is faith that can make you to be in the Spirit despite what you are seeing in the physical.

"But without faith it is impossible to please him: for he that cometh to God must believe that he is and that he is a rewarder of them that diligently seek him". Hebrews 11:6 KJV

Without faith you cannot please God. Faith is very important in our walk with God.

"So then faith cometh by hearing and hearing by the word of God". Romans 10:17 KJV

It is what you hear that determines your reasoning and eventually what you become. Someone that hears words of failure always, he/she will be a failure if care is not taken. You need to be rooted in the word of God to keep your faith alive. The word of God and faith are related.

As one grows in the Lord, one's faith gets deeper through one's depth in the word of God and the experiences God has given one. May you increase in faith in Jesus name, Amen.

Longsuffering:

"Thou therefore endure hardness as a good soldier of Jesus Christ". 2Timothy 2:3 KJV

At salvation, a measure of the anointing for longsuffering is released upon one by which one could endure persecutions from the devil and his forces,

"Blessed are they which are persecuted for righteousness' sake: for theirs is the Kingdom of heaven"   Matthew 5:10 KJV

Every child of God must face persecution from the devil, so God has placed in us the grace we need to be able to overcome the persecutions of the devil.

Gentleness:

"Behold, I send you forth as sheep in the midst of wolves: be ye therefore wise as serpents and harmless as doves".   Matthew 10:16 KJV

"Wherefore, my beloved brethren, let every man be swift to hear, slow to speak, slow to wrath". James 1:19 KJV

At salvation, a measure of the anointing of gentleness is released upon one by which one handle things calmly and relate kindly with people. A child of God should not be known to be harsh.

Goodness:

"Let your light so shine before men, that they may see your good works and glorify your Father which is in heaven". Matthew 5:16 KJV

At salvation, a measure of the anointing to do good is placed upon us. As children of God, we are the light of the World and God expected us to shine upon the Earth through our good works. Every child of God must be doing good anywhere he/she is.

Meekness:

"Blessed are the meek: for they shall inherit the earth". Matthew 5:5 KJV

At salvation, the grace for meekness is released upon us. Humility is a very important virtue a child of God must have. You must humble yourself before God so that God can use one to His glory.

"For whosoever exalteth himself shall be abased; and he that humbleth himself shall be exalted". Luke 14:11 KJV

According to the scripture above, it shows that we must humble ourselves always, so that God can exalt us. No child of God should be proud because pride is from the devil. It is when you humble yourself before God that you will be able to glorify God and then get His blessings abundantly into your life. Anyone that is not humble is not yet saved or his salvation is not complete. It is when you humble yourself before God that you will be able to obey Him. Also, we are to live a humble life.

Temperance:

"All things are lawful unto me but all things are not expedient: all things are lawful for me but I will not be brought under the power of any. Meats for the belly and the belly for meats: but God shall destroy both it and them. Now the body is not for fornication but for the Lord and the Lord for the body". 1Corinthians 6:12-13 KJV

"And every man that striveth for the mastery is temperate in all things. Now they do it to obtain a corruptible crown but we an incorruptible". ICorrinthians 9:25 KJV

At salvation, the grace of temperance is upon us which makes us to discipline our bodies from the acts of the flesh which might want to fall us. Every child of God must have self control. The devil sets traps through the flesh and it is this virtue of temperance that will help one to overcome such traps of the devil.

In Daniel 1:1-16, Daniel disciplined himself not to defile himself with the delicacy of the king's food which he knows could affect his body system. Some people have missed their purpose in life because of food.

In Genesis 39:7-12, Joseph disciplined his body as he stood

against the seduction of his master's wife. If he had fallen into the seduction, he would have missed the purpose of God for his life. Though he suffered for being self-disciplined but at the end, the purpose of God for his life came to pass.

As children of God that want to fulfill the purpose of God, we must have self-control or else one will fall into the trap of the enemy.

May the fruit of the Spirit be in full manifestation upon your life from now in Jesus name, Amen.

CHAPTER TWO

Water Baptism

"He shall put on the holy linen coat and he shall have the linen breeches upon his flesh and shall be girded with a linen girdle and with the linen mitre shall he be attired: these are holy garments; therefore shall he wash his flesh in water and so put them on".   Leviticus 16:4 KJV

God asked Moses to tell Aaron that he shall appear before Him in the Holy of Holies once in a year on the Day of Atonement, the 10th day of the 7th Hebrew month. During the Day of Atonement, Aaron shall intercede for the children of Israel for their forgiveness before God. He shall first purify himself. He was asked to wash himself with water before putting on his holy garment. This washing of Aaron with water is a symbolism of water baptism.

"Moreover, brethren, I would not that ye should be ignorant, how that all our fathers were under the cloud and passed through the sea. And were all baptized unto Moses in the cloud and in the sea".   1Corinthians 10:1-2 KJV

The crossing of the Red Sea by the children of Israel when God liberated them from Egypt is also a symbolism of Water Baptism. As they went through the Red Sea, they got their victory over the Pharaoh and the host of Egypt who were buried in the Red Sea. The crossing of the Red Sea was a form of salvation for the children of Israel from their oppressors.

Also according to Joshua chapters 4 and 5, after the Lord parted the River Jordan and the children of Israel crossed it as it was with the Red Sea, they came to Gilgal where the reproach of Egypt was rolled away from them. The crossing of the River Jordan is also a symbolism of Water Baptism for the children of Israel.

"And he came into all the country about Jordan, preaching the baptism of repentance for the remission of sins".   Luke 3:3 KJV

God always make us to have a physical view of the spiritual things He wants to do. In the Old Testament, He established different physical things so that we could have the spiritual understanding which the New Testament reveals. The Old Testament is a shadow of things to come.

For example, God gave the children of Israel the feast of Passover in the Old Testament so that they and also we, who are saved through the blood of Jesus, could have the understanding of Jesus as the Passover Lamb.

As Jesus was to begin His Ministry, God first made John, the Baptist, to prepare the way for Him through the Water Baptism which is a symbolism of salvation through Christ. Through the Water Baptism, the people will have a better understanding of salvation through Christ. John, the Baptist, himself made the Jews to know that there is One who is coming after him that shall baptize them with the Holy Spirit and fire.

"Buried with him in baptism, wherein also ye are risen with him through the faith of the operation of God, who hath raised him from the dead". Colossians 2:12 KJV

Water Baptism is an outward act that symbolizes repentance and faith in Christ i.e. a symbolism of salvation. As one is dipped under the water, it symbolizes the death and burial of Jesus Christ. As one is raised out of the water, it symbolizes the resurrection of Jesus from the grave. Under the water is one's old dead life and out of the water is one's new life which has been cleansed by the blood of Jesus. Water Baptism is a symbol of salvation. One could take water baptism and not get saved if one does not connect in the Spirit to the actual salvation. I have discussed salvation in Chapter One. For one that has already been saved, the water baptism just gives him/her a better understanding of what happened during his/her salvation.

"For by grace are ye saved through faith and that not of yourselves: it is the gift of God: Not of works, lest any man should boast".
Ephesians 2:8-9 KJV

Also read Romans 3:28, Galatians 2:16, Philippians 3:9.

Salvation is by divine grace through faith alone. Water baptism is not a requirement of salvation since no external act is necessary for salvation. You are saved through being born of the Spirit. I have explained John 3:3-6 in the Introduction.

"Go ye therefore and teach all nations, baptizing them in the name of the Father and of the Son and of the Holy Ghost".   Matthew 28:19 KJV

Jesus commanded His disciples when He was ascending to Heaven to baptize people in the name of the Father, of the Son and of the Holy Spirit. The commandment still holds till today. We ought to take Water Baptism till today. As I have said, someone that is saved through the blood of Jesus via confession of his/her sin, if he/she takes water baptism, it will make him/her to have a better understanding of the salvation he/she has got. The water baptism is not the salvation but symbolism of salvation.

"And he said unto them, Go ye into all the world and preach the gospel to every creature. **He that believeth and is baptized shall be saved**

but he that believeth not shall be damned. And these signs shall follow them that believe; In my name shall they cast out devils; they shall speak with new tongues; They shall take up serpents and if they drink any deadly thing, it shall not hurt them; they shall lay hands on the sick and they shall recover". Mark 16:15-18 KJV

This is the account of the gospel of Mark about what Jesus told His disciples when He was ascending to Heaven as it was in Matthew 28:18-20. In that Mark 16:15-18, two experiences were mentioned: believed and baptized. Whoever that believes in Jesus has confessed Him as his/her Lord and Saviour (Romans 10:9-11). Such person is said to be saved and he/she is called a believer. Therefore, Mark 16:16 talks about salvation through the blood of

Jesus and the water baptism. Then the later part of the verse 16 says whoever that didn't believe shall be damned i.e. whoever that doesn't have salvation through the blood of Jesus shall be damned. It was not said that whoever that didn't have water baptism shall be damned. I have said, the water baptism gives us an understanding of the salvation we have got through the blood of Jesus and that is why the early part of verse 16 reveals that after one has got the salvation through the blood of Jesus i.e. believed, then one will do the water baptism to get the better understanding of the salvation one has got.

The verses 17-18 reveal the signs that shall follow those who are saved through the blood of Jesus i.e. believers. Once you are saved through the blood of Jesus, those signs shall follow you either you are baptized or not.

"To him give all the prophets witness, **that through his name whoever believeth in him shall receive remission of sins**. While Peter yet spake these words, the Holy Ghost fell on all them which heard the word" Acts 10:43-44 KJV

Peter was sent by the Lord to the house of Cornelius to minister salvation to his household. We saw that after Peter had declared salvation through the blood of Jesus to them and they have believed, then the signs that follow those that believed, followed them as the Holy Spirit came upon them and they spoke with tongues (Acts 10:45-46).

It was after the baptism of the Holy Spirit that Peter did the water baptism for them to make them to have a better understanding of the salvation they got through the blood of Jesus. For someone to be filled with the Holy Spirit, it means that God has accepted him/her as His own and that came upon them after their salvation through the blood of Jesus. This shows the importance of the salvation through the blood of Jesus. I too had the Holy Spirit baptism before I later did the water baptism after many years.

Water baptism is not required to make Heaven as I have explained in the Introduction. What is required to make heaven is your salvation and continuous walk with the Lord to the end.

Water baptism should be carried out in a flowing river and should be taken by someone that has reached the level that he/she could confess his/her sin and able to live a holy life by himself. Water baptism should not be done on infant or by sprinkling of water on the person or in a swimming pool. Everyone that did water baptism in the New Testament, did it in a flowing river.

Great caution must be taken whenever water baptism is to be taken in the flowing river. Rivers are under the influence of Marine powers and the devil knowing the symbolic meaning of the water baptism always contend against the activity. Both the Pastors and the people to be baptized must be spiritually sensitive during the water baptism. The water area should be sanctified before the baptism and importantly, the Church should be led by the Holy Spirit to do the water baptism. Most times, we turn water baptism into normal events. Holy Spirit must lead the Church to carry out the water baptism and by that the program shall be perfectly done both spiritually and physically.

Some people have gone for water baptism in a flowing river and came back with the contamination of evil spirit into them. I know of a sister who went for water baptism conducted by her Church in a flowing river and the night after the water baptism, she had a terrible dream that I began to pray for her deliverance. I am not saying this to scare you about water baptism but just letting you know how you need to be spiritually sensitive when you are going for water baptism. I too did water baptism around 1998/1999 and I was excited in the Spirit when I did it. Water baptism is important but it is not a requirement for salvation.

People that did water baptism in the New Testament

1. Jesus Christ (Luke 3:21-22)
2. Paul (Acts 22:16).
3. Cornelius (Acts 10:48).
4. Ethiopia Eunuch (Acts 8:36-38).

CHAPTER
THREE
Sanctification

"Sanctify them through thy truth: thy word is truth".   John 17:17 KJV

"But as he which hath called you is holy, so be ye holy in all manner of conversation. Because it is written, Be ye holy; for I am holy". 1Peter 1:15-16 KJV

"Sanctify yourself therefore and ye be holy: for I am the LORD your God. And ye shall keep my statues and do them: I am the LORD which sanctify you".   Leviticus 20:7-8 KJV

Sanctification means holiness. It is the state where the root of sin, the root of the Adamic sin is uprooted from one e.g. the root of stubbornness, drunkenness, fornication, smoking etc. After salvation, one needs to get to this state for one to have the Holy Spirit Baptism, the outpouring of the Holy Spirit upon one. Sanctification is a grace, that is, it is an anointing. Only God can make you holy.

"Thou art of pure eyes than to behold evil and cannot look on iniquity" Habakkuk 1:13 KJV

God cannot anoint filthy vessels, so before He places His anointing upon us, He first purifies us. Before one can have the Holy Spirit Baptism, one must first be sanctified. After the sanctification, then one can be baptized by the Holy Spirit.

Everyone that God has anointed for service (Ministry) was first sanctified before the anointing fell upon them. We shall look at some of the people anointed by God:

"And when the LORD saw that he turned aside to see, God called unto him out of the midst of the bush and said Moses. And he said, Here am I. and he said, Draw not nigh hither: put off thy shoes from off thy feet, for the place whereon thou standest is holy ground".   Exodus 3:4-5 KJV

God appeared to Moses, as he led the sheep of his father-in-law through Mount Sinai, in a bush burning with fire and the bush was not consumed. As Moses turned to see, God called him and told him to remove his shoes for the place is holy. Through the removal of his shoes, Moses was sanctified by God which then qualified him for being anointed by God.

"And the LORD said unto Moses, Go unto the people and sanctify them today and tomorrow and let them wash their clothes. And be ready against the third day for the third day, the LORD will come down in the sight of all the people upon Mount Sinai"   Exodus 19:10-11 KJV

After the children of Israel had been liberated from Egypt and brought into the wilderness, at Mount Sinai, the LORD wanted to reveal Himself to them. The presence of God around us is the anointing. God told Moses to tell the people to sanctify themselves for two days and that they should wash their clothes. The third day, God shall appear to them. The washing of their clothes and separation from defiling things sanctified them and qualified them to experience the presence of God.

"And Joshua said unto the people, sanctify yourselves: for tomorrow the LORD will do wonders among you".   Joshua 3:5 KJV

When God was to give the children of Israel Canaanland through a warfare, as they prepared to cross River Jordan, Joshua asked them to sanctify themselves because God shall be coming in their midst as the priests shall bear the Ark of Covenant for the River Jordan to part. They sanctified themselves and the presence of the LORD parted the River Jordan for them as they went through to the other side.

"And when the day of Pentecost was fully come, they were all with one accord in one place. And suddenly there came a sound from heaven as of a rushing mighty wind and it filled all the house where they were sitting. And there appeared unto them cloven tongues like as of fire and it sat upon each of them. And they were all filled with the Holy Ghost and began to speak with other tongues as the Spirit gave them utterance" Acts 2:1-4 KJV

Jesus had commanded His disciples to wait in Jerusalem until they were endued with power, then they will witness for Him everywhere. They waited in the upper room. When you wait on the Lord, you are praying and fasting. We get sanctified through praying and sometimes added with fasting. Therefore, the disciples became sanctified in the upper room and on the day of Pentecost, the outpouring of the Holy Spirit fell upon them and they began to preach everywhere to people.

"Now there were in the church that was at Antioch certain prophets and teachers; as Barnabas and Simeon that was called Niger and

Lucius of Cyrene and Manaen which had been brought up with Herod, the tetrarch and Saul. As they ministered to the Lord and fasted, the Holy Ghost said separate me Barnabas and Saul for the work whereunto I have called them". Acts 13:1-2 KJV

As the five people in the scripture above were fasting and praying i.e. consecrating themselves unto God, the anointing for separation fell upon Paul and Barnabas to separate them as Apostles to the Gentiles.

You have seen how the grace of sanctification (consecration) is important for anointing to come upon one. If you are born again and you are seeking the Holy Spirit baptism, you must first be sanctified before you can be baptized by the Holy Spirit. Seek for the grace of sanctification and the Lord shall give it to you.

"Or what man is there of you whom if his son ask bread will he give him a stone? Or if he ask of fish, will he give him a serpent? If ye then, being evil, know how to give good gifts unto your children, how much more shall your Father which is in heaven give good things to them that ask him?" Matthew 7:9-11 KJV

You can ask for the grace of sanctification and God shall sanctify you, only if you ask with genuine heart.

<u>Why do we need to be sanctified</u>

1. For our worship to be accepted (1Peter 2:5,9, 1Thessalonians 4:7).

2. To have access to the presence of God (Hebrews 12:14, Psalm 24:3-6, Exodus 19:10-25, Revelation 4:8, Isaiah 6:3, Obadiah 1:17).
3. To be rapture (Colossians 1:20-22, Ephesians 2:20-21, Ephesians 5:26-27, 1Corinthians 3:17).

How to get sanctified

1. Be born again (John 3:3).
2. Present yourself holy unto God (Romans 12:1-2, 2Corinthians 7:1).
3. Ask God to sanctify you i.e. knowing that sanctification is a power from God (John 17:17, Colossians 1:20-22).

"And Zacchaeus stood and said; Behold, Lord, the half of my goods I give to the poor; and if I have taken any thing from any man by false accusation, I restore him fourfold".Luke 19:8 KJV

At times, restitution is needed before one could be sanctified. Restitution is returning back what you have falsely taken from people before salvation or confession of the sin you have committed against people, unknown to the people committed them against, before your salvation. Holy Spirit must lead you to do restitution. You should not do restitution on your own but under the leading of the Holy Spirit.

"Confess your faults one to another and pray one for another, that ye may be healed. The effectual fervent prayer of a righteous man availeth much". James 5:16 KJV

Any sin that you have confessed before God and has fully cleared from your mind, you may not need restitution for such. If after your salvation, any sin which you have confessed is still troubling your mind and you have prayed severally about the sin but could not clear out of your mind, then such could be confessed before the people you have done them against but you must ask for the leading of the Holy Spirit. At times, devil might just be trying to hold such sin against one and just need to bind the devil concerning such and you gain your victory.

"There is therefore now no condemnation to them which are in Christ Jesus, who walk not after the flesh but after the Spirit". Romans 8:1 KJV

Once you are truly saved, there is no condemnation against you about your past. If restitution is needed to be taken by you, the Holy Spirit shall lead you into it. Every spiritual task is to be taken through the leading of the Holy Spirit. Always submit yourself to the leading of the Holy Spirit and He will teach and direct you about what to do at all time.

It is time to go and seek the face of God in prayer:

1. Ask for the forgiveness of your sin.
2. Ask God to uproot the roots of sin from you i.e. ask for the release of the power of sanctification upon you. You can mention the sins you want God to uproot from you if you know them or you pray

generally for the uprooting of the Adamic sin from you.
3. Ask God for the grace to live in holiness forever.
4. Ask God for the grace to always follow the leading of the Holy Spirit.
5. Thank God for the answered prayers.

CHAPTER FOUR

Holy Spirit Baptism

"He that believeth on me, as the scripture hath said, out of his belly shall flow rivers of living water". John 7:38 KJV.

The Holy Spirit Baptism is also called the outpouring of the Holy Spirit. It is a greater measure of the anointing than the indwelling anointing. It makes you a blessing to others. It is the anointing needed to fulfill the calling God has called one into. The anointing comes upon one when it is needed for service i.e. when needed to fulfill the call of God upon one. It is in measure upon us according to the grace of God in our lives. It was on Jesus without measure (John 3:34).

Anyone called into Ministry must have the outpouring of the Holy Spirit on him/her before he/she can function effectively in the calling.

"Now Peter sat without in the palace and a damsel came unto him saying, thou also wast with Jesus of Galilee. But he denied before them all, saying I know not what thou sayest". Matthew 26:69-70 KJV

When Jesus was being tried by the high priest, a young girl came to Peter that he was with Jesus. Peter could not stand the young girl at that time. At that period of the disciples moving with Jesus before the day of Pentecost, they were only under the indwelling anointing. Peter couldn't withstand the persecution during the trial of Jesus because the anointing for service has not come upon them.

"And behold, I send the promise of my Father upon you: but tarry ye in the city of Jerusalem until ye be endued with power from on high". Luke 24:49 KJV

"But ye shall receive power; after that the Holy Ghost is come upon you and ye shall be witnesses unto me both in Jerusalem and in all Judea and in Samaria and unto the uttermost part of the Earth". Acts 1:8 KJV

When Jesus was ascending to heaven, He told His disciples to wait in Jerusalem till they are empowered with the Holy Spirit, then they will be able to be His witness everywhere. The disciples did as the Lord had commanded them as they waited in the upper room. I have said in the previous chapter that during their waiting in the upper room, they got sanctified. Then, on the day of the Pentecost, the baptism of the Holy Spirit came upon them and there was instant manifestation of the anointing upon them. The grace for boldness came upon them and they stood up as Peter ministered to the people. About 3,000 souls became saved that day. Whenever one is anointed, there will always be instant manifestation around one.

"But Peter and John answered and said unto them, whether it be right in the sight of God to

hearken unto you more than unto God, judge ye".
Acts 4:19 KJV

After the disciples had received the Holy Spirit baptism, Peter and John went to the temple. On their way to the temple, a lame man from birth begged them for alms but instead they healed him and he began to walk. The lame man followed Peter and John into the temple. This drew the attention of people to Peter and John. Peter began to preach to the people. As they spoke to the people, the priests, the captain of the temple and the Sadducees were annoyed with Peter and John. They arrested them. Though many of the people Peter and John had preached to, believed. In the next day, the high priest and others questioned the power that they have done the healing with. Peter and John under the anointing spoke boldly to them. The Peter that couldn't stand a young girl, can now stand the high priest. This was possible for Peter because he had been baptized by the Holy Spirit.

"And when they had prayed, the place was shaken where they were assembled together and they were all filled with the Holy Ghost and they spoke the word of God with boldness" Acts 4:31 KJV

After Peter and John were released, they went to meet the other disciples and told them what had happened. They prayed and the place was shaken. They then increased in anointing. You can increase in the outpouring anointing. You need a fresh anointing upon you every moment of your life.

Baptism of the Holy Spirit is accompanied by the speaking in tongues. The Holy Spirit will give one the utterance. You will speak freely as Holy Spirit gives you the utterance.

In July 1992 during our secondary school fellowship, as we the students gathered together for fellowship under the ministration of our immediate past senior, Brother Collins, during the prayer session, I was baptized with the Holy Spirit. I was the only student that was baptized in the fellowship that day. The outpouring anointing just came upon me as I was praying and I felt the anointing upon me. I began to speak in tongue. I was in senior secondary school two then at Bolade Grammar School, Oshodi, Lagos state, Nigeria. What a day in my life. From that day, I felt an unusual hunger to carry out the service of God. I could feel in me the anointing for service. If you also want the Holy Spirit baptism, God can release His Spirit upon you for His service.

Ministry Gifts

"And **he gave some apostles; and some prophets; and some evangelist; and some pastors; and some teachers**; for the perfecting of the saints, for the work of the Ministry, for the edifying of the body of Christ: Till we all come in the unity of the faith and of the knowledge of the son of God, unto a perfect man, unto the measure of the stature of the fullness of Christ". Ephesians 4:11-13 KJV

Also read 1Corinthians 12:28, Romans 12:6-8 and Revelation 5:10.

The Anointing required to do the work of the Ministry is called the Ministry gifts. This Anointing makes us to stand in the office (Ministry) which God has called us into.

Apostolic Ministry:

This office is held by an Apostle. An Apostle is someone that is sent forth with a commission (John 20:21, Acts 13:1-3, Mark 16:15-18).

An Apostle has the following attributes:

a. Ability to manifest signs and wonders (2Corinthians 12:12).
b. Ability to establish churches (Ephesians 2:20).
c. Have a deeper personal experience with the Lord (Galatians 1:12, Acts 9:1-9, Acts 1:15-22).

Apostles are Missionaries. They are sent by God for a unique assignment. They take the gospel to a place and after winning souls there, plant a church. They nurture the planted church to maturity and leave for another place. Pastors are placed over the planted churches. They come regularly to see how the planted churches are doing.

Prophetic Ministry:

This office is held by a Prophet. A Prophet is a mouthpiece or spokesman of God. He declares what God is saying to people. He represents God before people. Whenever a prophet is declaring the word of God, he is not seeing the physical people around him but he is in the spirit seeing God that has sent him and the devil that might want to stop the move of God. He operates as the Angels of God operate whenever they bring messages to people. They could not tolerate any human weakness which makes humans want to doubt the spoken word. So, they always get angry in such cases except for the people that mercy spoke for (2Kings 7:1-20, Luke 1:5-22).

God declares His plans to mankind through His prophets either His blessings or judgment. After the fall of Adam and Eve which cut them from God, the need for God to choose people to talk through to people arose. Though now, in the New Testament, the Holy Spirit could talk to us directly but hidden plans of God are revealed by God through His prophets (Deuteronomy 29:29, Amos 3:7).

The roles of prophets are:

- a. God reveals His plans to them through revelations and visions (Hosea 12:10, Genesis 28:10-15, 2Chronicles 1:7-12, Exodus 3:1-22).

b. They liberate the captives (Hosea 12:13, Judges 6:1-24).
c. They help people to possess their possessions (Joshua 18:1-10, Genesis 14:1-16, 1Samuel 30:16-20).
d. They bless people (Deuteronomy 33:1-29).
e. They break curses and evil covenants (Genesis 49:3-4, Deuteronomy 33:1-6, 2Kings 2:19-22).
f. They restore what has been lost (2Kings 6:1-7).
g. They curse and judge (2Kings 2:23-24, Numbers 16:1-35).

Priesthood Ministry:

This office is held by a priest. A priest represents people before God. He speaks on behalf of people before God. He is an intercessor. This is the opposite of the role of a prophet.

The High priest enters into the Holy of holies once in a year, the Day of Atonement (10th day in the seventh Hebrew month), to offer sacrifice for the sin of himself and of the entire children of Israel. Jesus is our High priest who entered once into the heavenly Holy of holies to present His blood for the remission of our sin (Hebrews 9:1-28).

The roles of the priests are:

a. To offer sacrifices unto God (Leviticus 6:8-23, 2Chronicles 7:1-7).
b. Teach people the laws of God i.e. they are teachers of the words of God (2Chronicles 15:3, Ezra 7:6-10).
c. They call people to salvation (Ezra 10:10-19).
d. They lay the foundation of people in God and dedicate the Temple (1Samuel 1:9-18, 1Samuel 2:20-21, 2Chronicles 5:11-14, Hebrews 9:7).
e. Give directions to the people of God (1Samuel 30:7-8).
f. Intercede for people (Exodus 32:30-33, Numbers 14:11-20).

g. Take care of the house of God (1Chronicles 26:1-12)
h. Lead worship in the house of God (1Chronicles 25:1-7).

A priest stands in gap between God and man asking for the mercy of God upon mankind through the blood of Jesus.

Evangelical Ministry:

This office is held by an Evangelist. An Evangelist preaches salvation to people. He organises revival services in the Church. He is eager to win souls into the Kingdom of God (Acts 21:8-9, Acts 8:5-40).

Pastoral Ministry:

This office is held by a Pastor. A Pastor feed the flocks of Christ. He is a shepherd that takes care of the sheep in a Church of God (Acts 20:28, Jeremiah 3:15).

Teaching Ministry:

This office is held by a Teacher. A teacher teaches the word of God (Matthew 5:1-2).

Helps Ministry:

This Ministry assists the main Ministries to carry out their functions. These are burdens bearers. Examples of the Helps

Ministry in the Church are Choirs, Ushers, Deacons etc. (Acts 6:1-8).

"And are built upon the foundation of the Apostles and Prophets, Jesus Christ himself being the chief corner stone". Ephesians 2:20 KJV

The foundation of the Church, either the first Church (the early Church) or any local Churches these days, are laid by Apostles and Prophets. God still anoint people into the office of the Apostles till now.

The foundation of any local Church these days can only be laid by Prophets and Apostles. If there is no Prophet and Apostle in the Church that wants to plant a new Church and God gave the order for the planting of the new Church, then God will temporarily place Apostolic and Prophetic anointing on any of the Pastor, Teacher or Evangelist present for the actualisation of the task. As it is in a secular organisation where people could perform in an acting capacity whenever the person to hold a position is not around.

A Prophet spiritually clears the environment as a builder must first clear the bush on a land before they can build on it. Then the Apostle spiritually lays the foundation stones on the spiritually cleared environment. Whenever the spiritual requirements needed for any task is fulfilled, then there must be results.

The Apostles are very important in the Church till now. To have a better understanding of divine calling, you can read my book titled: "Understanding divine calling: a launch into the supernatural realm".

Only Jesus can choose Apostles, no one can choose or anoint one to stand in the office of the Apostles. Barnabas and Paul were chosen directly by God to stand in the office of the Apostles (Acts 13:1-2).

Pastors, Teachers and Evangelists can be chosen and anointed by Pastors, Teachers and Evangelists respectively and the anointing to stand in each offices rest on the people to function in the offices.

But Apostles, Prophets and Priests are chosen directly by God. God choose by Himself who shall be His mouthpiece. No

Prophet can choose anyone to stand in the office of the Prophets. Elijah didn't choose Elisha. God anointed Elisha by Himself through the fallen mantle He had placed upon Elijah. Elisha only learnt administrative activities from Elijah. Same thing with Joshua who succeeded Moses.

Also, God choose by Himself who shall stand before Him on behalf of people. One could learn administrative work from the older Apostles, Prophets and Priests but God places the people in those offices by Himself. God anoints people directly by Himself to bring people into the offices of Apostles, Prophets and Priests.

Whatever Ministry you are called into, you need anointing to be able to function in it effectively.

Spiritual gifts

"Now concerning spiritual gifts, brethren, I would not have you ignorant. Ye know that ye were Gentiles, carried away unto those dumb idols even as ye were led. Wherefore, I give you to understand that no man speaking by the Spirit of God calleth Jesus accursed: and that no man can say that Jesus is the Lord but by the Holy Ghost. Now there are differences of administrations but the same Lord. And there are diversities of operations but the same God which worketh in all. But the manifestation of the Spirit is given to every man to profit withal. For to one is given by the Spirit, the word of wisdom; to another the word of knowledge by the same Spirit. To another faith by the same Spirit; to another the gifts of healing by the same Spirit. To another the working of miracles; to another prophecy; to another discerning of spirits; to another divers kinds of tongues; to another the interpretation of tongues: But all these worketh that one and the selfsame Spirit diving to every man severally as he will". 1Corinthians 12:1-11 KJV

Spiritual gifts are the anointing that one needs to be able to function in the office(s) e.g. the anointing that a Pastor need to be able to function.

Spiritual gift of the word of wisdom:

This is the anointing to have the understanding of events. It involves speaking hidden truths of what is not known.

Spiritual gift of the word of knowledge:

This is the revelation about things i.e. God given one a word of knowledge about a particular situation or person in order to guide or warn the person e.g. Paul warning the crew of the ship when he was being taken to Rome to be tried and he told them not to sail yet but they didn't listen and later storm came against the ship but Paul still gave them the word of knowledge that no life shall be lost (Acts 27).

Spiritual gift of faith:

This is different from the faith of the fruit of the Spirit which all believers have. The gift of faith involves the supernatural endowment to believe and trust God in difficult situations which then birth extraordinary results. This is the measure of faith exhibited by David when he fought Goliath. Also by Daniel when thrown into the lions' den; Shadrach, Meshach and Abednego when thrown into the fiery furnace in Babylon. It is a greater measure of faith than faith by the fruit of the Spirit that comes into us at salvation.

Spiritual gifts of healing:

This is the anointing to heal the sick and set the captives free.

Spiritual gift of working of miracles:

This is the anointing to carry out supernatural miracles e.g. the walking of Jesus on the Sea, the shadow of Peter healing the sick etc.

Spiritual gift of prophecy:

This gift reveals the future. It helps the Church to know the mind of God. The gift of prophecy is different from the anointing of the prophet. The anointing of the prophet is a greater measure of anointing which is only upon the prophets but any believers can be filled with the gift of prophecy to edify, exhort and comfort the

Church according to 1Corinthians 14:3.

Spiritual gift of discerning of spirits:

This gift helps to know whether a situation or person is good or bad, right or wrong, Godly or demonic. This gift is very important in the Church to reveal the agents of darkness parading themselves as the children of God.

Spiritual gift of different kinds of tongue:

This is the gift that empowers one to speak in unknown (heavenly) tongues and known (earthly) tongues.

Spiritual gift of the interpretation of tongues:

This gift helps to understand and explain (interpret) to others the words spoken in unknown (heavenly) tongues.

The two rains

"Fear not, O land, be glad and rejoice: for the LORD will do great things. Be not afraid, ye beasts of the field: for the pastures of the wilderness do spring, for the tree beareth her fruit, the fig tree and the vine to yield their strength. Be glad then ye children of Zion and rejoice in the LORD your God: for he hath given you the former rain moderately and he will cause to come down for you the rain, the former rain and the latter rain in the first month. And the floors shall be full of wheat and the fats shall overflow with wine and oil. And I will restore to you the years that the locust hath eaten, the cankerworm and the caterpillar, and the palmerworm, my great army which I sent among you. And ye shall eat in plenty and be satisfied and praise the name of the LORD your God that hath dealt wondrously with you: and my people shall never be ashamed: And ye shall know that I am in the midst of Israel and that I am the LORD your God and none else and my people shall never be ashamed. And it shall come to pass afterward that I will pour out my Spirit upon all flesh and your sons and daughters shall prophesy, your old men shall dream dreams, your young men shall see visions. And also upon the servants and upon the handmaids in those days will I pour out my Spirit" Joel 2:21-29 KJV

God has plans for every generation and the anointing to fulfill the plans of God for that generation is always released upon the people He has chosen to fulfill His plans for the generation.

Anointing can be upon an individual or upon a group of people united for a purpose e.g. Church. This anointing upon a group of people is greater than an individual anointing on each members of the group. There is an anointing that a generation carries to fulfill the plans of God for that generation and this anointing is greater than the individual anointing on each person in that generation:

The former rain:

Rain represents anointing. In the Joel 2:21-29, two rains were mentioned: the former rain and the latter rain. The former rain was fulfilled on the day of Pentecost. The former rain came down moderately to show the level of the anointing on the day of Pentecost when compared with the latter rain. This former rain launched out the early Church and the floors were full of wheat and the fats overflowed with wine and oil which were the harvested souls that the anointing produced. The first harvest of 3,000 souls was won into the Church and the kingdom of God.

The latter rain:

This is the second rain in Joel 2:21-29 and this rain is heavier than the former rain i.e. the anointing of the latter rain is greater than the former rain. The latter rain shall launch out the End time Church that will prepare the way of the Lord Jesus for His second coming. The anointing on the End time Church shall be greater than that on the early Church (Haggai 2:1-9).

The latter rain is characterized by floods so the end time Church shall be under the greater measure of anointing that can uproot the powers of hell greatly.

As the early Church was launched out by the former rain, so also, we, the End time Church is waiting spiritually in the spiritual upper room for the coming of the latter rain which shall launch out the End time Church.

The launch of the End time Church is the start of the final harvest which will end on the day of rapture when saints shall be harvested into Heaven.

What to do to experience the baptism of the Holy Spirit

1. Be born again (John 3:16, Romans 10:8-10, Romans 10:13).
2. Be sanctified i.e. be holy (Hebrews 12:14, Hebrews 10:10-14, 1Peter 1:15-16, 1Peter 2:9-12)
3. Wait on the Lord in the upper room i.e. seek the

face of God in prayer (Luke 24:49, Acts 1:8-13, Matthew 17:14-21,Isaiah40:28-31, Habakkuk 2:1-3).
4. Be in unity i.e. live in love (Acts 1:14, Acts 2:1-13, 1Corinthians 14:33, John 17:20-23).

How to remain under the anointing

1. Declare God boldly to people (Acts 2:14-36, Acts 4:1-22, Luke 9:26).
2. Be fruitful (Acts 2:37-41, Acts 3:1-11, Matthew 13:8).
3. Return all the glory to God as the doer of every work (Acts 3:12-20).
4. Constantly fellowship with brethren to pray and study the word of God together

(Acts 2:42-47, Acts 4:31-37, Hebrews 10:25).

It is time to seek the face of God in prayer:

1. Sing some praise/worship songs unto God.
2. Ask God for the forgiveness of your sin.
3. Ask God to make you holy.
4. Ask God for the grace to always wait on Him.
5. Ask God to give you the grace to live in love.
6. Ask God for the Baptism of the Holy Spirit upon you.
7. Ask God for the grace to boldly declare Him to people.
8. Ask God for the grace of fruitfulness to be released upon you.

9. Ask God for the grace to always glorify God.
10. Ask God for the grace to constantly fellowship with brethren.
11. Thank God for the answered prayer.

Please, be in the Spirit now:

Holy Spirit, I surrender this Your child unto You, reveal Yourself to him/her and let him/her experience Your baptism in Jesus name, Amen.

For counseling, prayer or to share your testimony, you can contact the author through:

Email: sundayakodu@yahoo.com

Telephone: +2348024996245

Other books by the author

1. **A victorious spiritual warfare:** using my testimony as a case study.
2. **Faith that works:** the building of a living faith.
3. **Deliverance from bondage:** a launch into the realm of a conqueror.
4. **Understanding the End time events:** a revelation into divine mysteries.
5. **The Temple of God:** a launch into the realm of revival.
6. **Understanding divine calling:** a launch into the supernatural realm.
7. **Fulfilling the purpose of God:** becoming who God

has created you on the Earth.
8. **The 12th Apostle of the Lamb:** the replacement of Judas Iscariot.
9. **The Holy Trinity:** a launch into the realm of open heavens.

About the Book

This book came through the inspiration of the Holy Spirit to open the Church to a better understanding of Water and the Holy Spirit Baptism. We are in the perilous times and the major tool the devil and his forces are using to fight the Church is to cut the Church from having the deeper knowledge of the word of God as they know that our victories lie in our knowledge of the word of God. We can only overcome the devil through the word of God, so the need for us to have the deeper knowledge of the word of God.

We are in the period when the forces of hell are shaking the entire world with different attacks. You, as a child of God too need to get yourself equipped to be able to withstand the trials that this period entail. The purpose of this book is to guide you into the realm of experiencing the power of God upon you so that you can stand against any attacks from the pit of hell.

I believe you shall experience the outpouring of the Holy Spirit upon you as you read through this book with total sensitivity in the Spirit. Be blessed.